W9-ACH-317

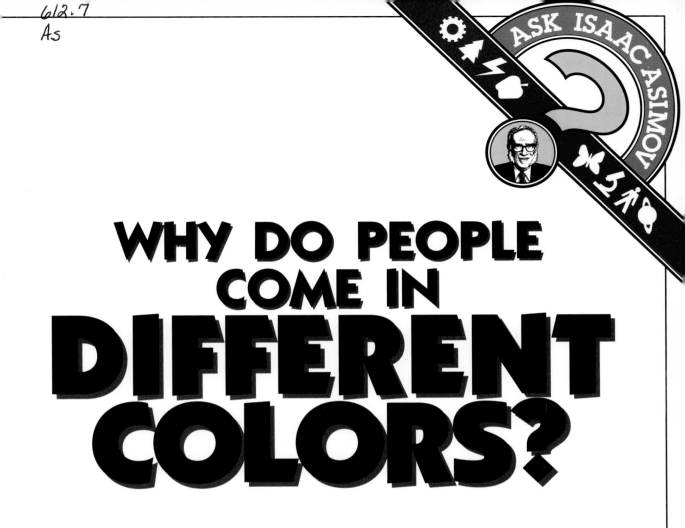

ASK ISAAC ASIMOV

WHY DO PEOPLE COME IN DIFFERENT COLORS?

BY ISAAC ASIMOV AND CARRIE DIERKS

Gareth Stevens Publishing
MILWAUKEE

For a free color catalog describing Gareth Stevens's list of high-quality children's books, call 1-800-341-3569 (USA) or 1-800-461-9120 (Canada).

The editor would like to thank Robert A. Rosen, M.D., of Newtowne Medical Group, Milwaukee, Wisconsin, for his assistance with the accuracy of the text; and Daniel Szeflinski, Jr., and Mark Garnaas for their assistance with the accuracy of the artwork.

The book designer would like to thank the models, Stephanie, Sam, Ray Jr., Bob, David, KyLee, and the Talavera family for their participation. Special thanks to Teri Kraus for the casting and logistics.

Library of Congress Cataloging-in-Publication Data

Asimov, Isaac, 1920-
    Why do people come in different colors? / by Isaac Asimov and
Carrie Dierks.
        p. cm. -- (Ask Isaac Asimov)
    Includes bibliographical references and index.
    Summary: Explains, in simple terms, the reasons for skin color,
how it is determined by heredity, and how various environmental
factors affect it.
    ISBN 0-8368-0808-8
    1. Color of man--Physiological aspects--Juvenile literature.
2. Melanin--Juvenile literature. 3. Skin--Physiology--Juvenile
literature. [1. Color of man. 2. Melanin. 3. Skin.] I. Dierks,
Carrie. II. Title. III. Series: Asimov, Isaac, 1920- Ask Isaac
Asimov.
QP88.5.A83 1993
612.7'927--dc20   93-20157

Edited, designed, and produced by
Gareth Stevens Publishing
1555 North RiverCenter Drive, Suite 201
Milwaukee, Wisconsin 53212, USA

At this time, Gareth Stevens, Inc., does not use 100 percent recycled paper, although the paper used in our books does contain about 30 percent recycled fiber. This decision was made after a careful study of current recycling procedures revealed their dubious environmental benefits. We will continue to explore recycling options.

Picture Credits
pp. 2-3, Kurt Carloni/Artisan, 1993; pp. 4-5, © D. D. Bryant/H. Armstrong Roberts; pp. 6-7, Kurt Carloni/Artisan, 1993; pp. 8-9, © Hutchison Library; pp. 10-11, © Jon Allyn, Cr. Photog., 1993; pp. 12-13, Courtesy of the American Red Cross; pp. 14-15, © Spaceshots/Earth Imaging; p. 14 (upper), © Bryan and CherryAlexander; p. 14 (lower), © K. Reno/H. Armstrong Roberts; p. 15 (left), © H. Armstrong Roberts; p. 15 (right), © A. Tovy/H. Armstrong Roberts; pp. 16-17, © Picture Perfect USA; pp. 18-19, © Bryan and Cherry Alexander; pp. 20-21, © Jon Allyn, Cr. Photog., 1993; pp. 22-23, © Bryan and Cherry Alexander; p. 24, © Bryan and Cherry Alexander

Cover photograph, © Jon Allyn, Cr. Photog., 1993: Various skin colors are made by a mere chemical called melanin. It produces more shades and tones than this ice cream!

Series editor: Barbara J. Behm
Series designer: Sabine Beaupré
Book designer: Kristi Ludwig
Art coordinator: Karen Knutson
Picture researcher: Diane Laska

Printed in the United States of America

1 2 3 4 5 6 7 8 9 98 97 96 95 94 93

Contents

Words that appear in the glossary are printed in **boldface** type the first time they occur in the text.

Learning about Your Body

Take a look at the many different people in the world around you. You will notice that human beings are all generally the same, but our bodies come in different "packages." Some people are short; some are tall. Some people are thin; some are wide. Some people have blond hair; some have red hair. Some people have brown eyes; some have blue. Skin also comes in many different colors. Our skin may be very dark or very light, or it may be somewhere in between. What do you think gives skin its color? Why do you think there are so many different colors of skin? Let's find out.

The Skin's Color Factory

Skin contains millions and millions of **cells.**
Cells are the basic units, or building blocks,
of all plants and animals. These cells are
constantly being produced and constantly
dying off. Most of the cells near the surface
of your skin are busy making new skin cells
to replace those that die and wear off. Some
of these cells produce **pigment**, a chemical
that gives things color. Skin color comes
from a pigment called **melanin**. Melanin
also gives your hair and eyes their color.

6

epidermis (outer layer of skin)

fat cells

dermis (inner layer of skin)

nerve

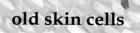

old skin cells

hair

sweat glands

blood vessels

From Light to Dark

Skin color varies because pigment cells produce different amounts of melanin. If your body produces a large amount of melanin, you have darker skin. If your body produces only a little melanin, you have lighter skin. Another reason for the various shades and tones of skin is a person's ability to tan. People who tan easily produce lots of melanin when exposed to sunlight. Other reasons include the thickness of a person's skin and the presence of the protein called **keratin**. People who produce *no* pigment have no color in their skin, hair, or eyes. This rare condition is called **albinism**.

Dots and Spots

Have you ever seen people who have **freckles**, **age spots**, or **moles**? Freckles are small spots of pigment located here and there on the skin. Some light-skinned people get freckles when they spend time in the Sun. Age spots often appear as people get

older and their bodies start producing
uneven amounts of melanin. Sometimes,
pigment cells group together and form a
dark clump called a mole. Most moles are
harmless. But a mole that changes color or
causes discomfort may need to be removed.

The Melanin Difference

For the most part, your body's ability to produce melanin is passed down from your parents. That's why children tend to have the same skin color as their parents, or some shade in between. Sunlight may also increase the amount of melanin present, causing skin to tan. Melanin protects the skin from sunburn by absorbing the Sun's invisible **ultraviolet rays**. Ultraviolet rays that are not absorbed can penetrate and burn the skin. It is a good idea to use sunscreen and wear a hat when you are in the Sun. This lowers the chance of developing wrinkles and skin cancer as you get older.

13

The First Humans

The earliest humans lived in Africa about one hundred thousand years ago. Most scientists believe they were dark skinned. By eleven thousand years ago, people had settled throughout the world.

Scientists believe light skin slowly came about as people moved into colder climates. The groups of people who lived in different parts of the world developed into different **races**. Races are groups of people that share similar traits, such as skin color, facial features, and body shape.

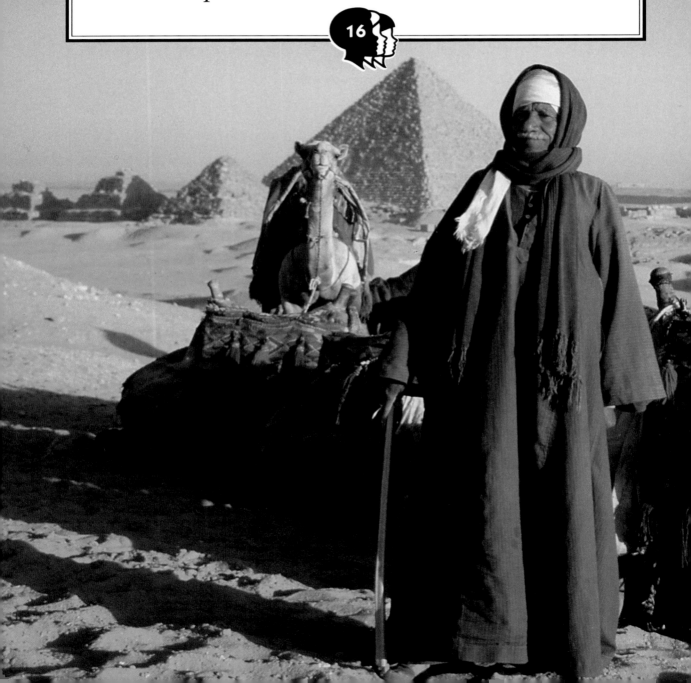

Surviving in Hot Climates

Many scientists think different skin colors have helped humans survive their different

16

climates. For instance, most people who originally came from hot, sunny climates near the equator have dark skin. Remember that melanin not only gives skin its color, it also absorbs harmful ultraviolet rays. In fact, the melanin in dark brown eyes even helps people see better in the Sun.

17

Surviving in Cold Climates

What about people who settled in the cold, cloudy areas of Earth? There is less Sun there, and the Sun's rays aren't as strong. Since there is less risk of skin damage from the Sun, people who lived in these areas didn't need to produce as much melanin. They could absorb sunlight for bone growth without damaging the skin. Over thousands of years, their skin became much lighter than the original humans.

18

The Changing Human Race

For much of human history, the different groups of people located throughout the world had little contact with one another. But over the past few hundred years, this has changed. Exploration, slavery, conflicts and wars, and modern transportation are just a few of the activities that have brought members of the different groups together. Often, members of one group choose mates from another. The children of these couples no longer have strict racial differences. Today, if you look at people from around the world, you will see an endless variety of skin colors and other features.

21

Color Is Skin Deep

Certain people have negative beliefs about skin color. For example, some people think that having a particular skin color makes them smarter or better than others. This is false. It is true that, at first glance, someone with a different skin color might seem very different from yourself. But keep in mind that skin color is caused by a mere chemical – melanin – with a little help from the Sun.

More Books to Read

The Skin by Alvin Silverstein and Virginia B. Silverstein
(Prentice-Hall)
What Color Are You? by Hal A. Franklin (Johnson
Publishing)
Your Skeleton and Skin by Ray Broekel (Childrens Press)
Your Skin and Hair by Joan Iveson-Iveson (Bookwright Press)
Your Skin Holds You In by Helen Grigsby Doss (Messner)

Places to Write

Here are some places you can write for more information. Be sure
to state exactly what you want to know. Give them your full name
and address so they can write back to you.

American Academy of
    Dermatology
P.O. Box 4014
Schaumburg, IL 60168-4014

International Society of
    Dermatology
200 1st Street, S.W.
Rochester, MN 55905

Institute for World
    Understanding of Peoples,
    Cultures, and Languages
939 Coast Boulevard - 19DE
La Jolla, CA 92037

Canadian Health Education
    Society
P.O. Box 2305, Stn. D
Ottawa, Ontario
K1P 5K0

Glossary

age spots: patches of skin that are darker than the rest of the skin
    due to uneven amounts of melanin being produced by the body
    as a person gets older.

albinism (AL-bin-ism): a condition in which a person's skin cells
    do not produce pigment, so the skin, hair, and eyes are
    colorless.

cells (sells): the smallest units, or building blocks, of living things.

freckles (FRECK-els): small spots on the skin caused by a greater amount of pigment than elsewhere on the skin.

keratin: (CARE-ah-tin): a protein found in skin, hair, and nails. This protein is found in people of all races.

melanin (MEL-uh-nin): the pigment that gives skin its color.

moles (mohls): small growths on the skin that are made up of clumps of pigment cells.

pigment (PIG-ment): a chemical that gives something its color.

races: groups of people that share a number of features, such as skin color and body shape.

ultraviolet rays (UL-truh-VYE-uh-let): invisible rays from the Sun that can cause sunburn.

Index